My details

Name: ______________________________

School: ______________________________

Favourite places: ______________________________

____

____

Favourite animals: ______________________________

____

____

Before you begin writing ...

Posture

1. Sit up straight at your table.
2. Put your feet flat on the floor.
3. Keep your wrist straight and resting on the table.

Pen grip

Left-handed

1. Rest the pen on your middle finger.
2. Pinch your index finger and thumb together gently.

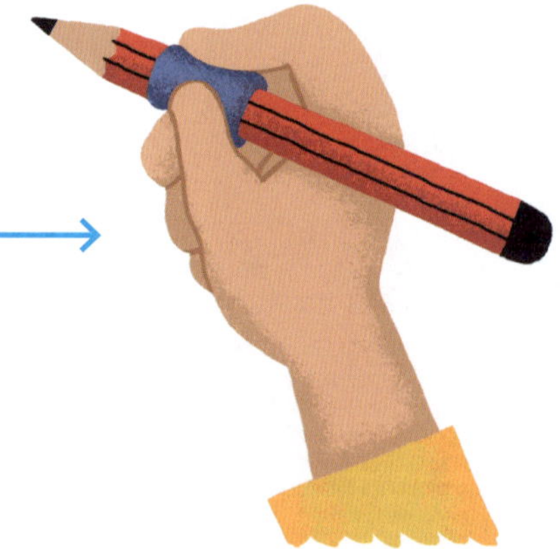

Right-handed

Paper

Left-handed

1. The paper is on an angle and held steady by your non-writing hand.
2. For right-handers, the page will tilt to the left.
3. For left-handers, the page will tilt to the right.

Right-handed

Revision

Letter formation

Before we start, let's revise the different types of handwriting. Remember that cursive handwriting is best for everyday writing and print handwriting is ideal for labelling maps and diagrams.

Copy these letters on the lines below. Then colour in the landscape.

A a B b C c D d E e F f G g H h I i

J j K k L l M m N n O o P p Q q R r

S s T t U u V v W w X x Y y Z z

In cursive handwriting, write your first and last name.

Copy these punctuation marks below:

. , “ ” ’ ? ! ; :

In cursive handwriting, write today's date.

In your neatest handwriting, copy the sentence below.

Excellent handwriting is easy to read.

Diagonal joins

Learning intention: To practise diagonal joins

Before you begin, complete the checklist below.

- ☐ I have my feet flat on the floor.
- ☐ My back is up nice and straight.
- ☐ I can hold my pen accurately.
- ☐ I can angle my paper correctly and use my non-writing hand to steady the page.

Tip! Remember to make your diagonal joins go directly to the next letter.

diagonal join

in

Practise your diagonal joins as you copy the letters, words and sentences below.

le ne in am du de ur er pi ly un ci

uc he ty is ky mi ui xe te li an ce

sustain life planet living ecosystem connected

intricate world animals plants organisms physical

food components system supports wildlife biosphere

The Earth's ecosystems form an interconnected web of living organisms and their physical environments. The physical environment includes both living organisms and non-living things, such as rocks, soil, minerals, water and sunlight.

OXFORD UNIVERSITY PRESS

Tip! Diagonal joins exit from the baseline directly to the next letter. After a diagonal join, the crossbar on the letter t goes above the join.

Remember, the letter t is slightly shorter than the other tall letters.

crossbar goes above the diagonal join

Practise your joins to and from the letter t as you copy the letters and sentences below.

it ut et tu ta at th te nt ti te ct

The ecosystems include all of the different organisms on Earth and their interaction with the physical environment. This includes both living and non-living things, which are connected and interdependent.

How many words can you find in the text above with a diagonal join from e to r? Write them below.

What does it look like where this fish lives? Finish the scene by adding the fish's surroundings.

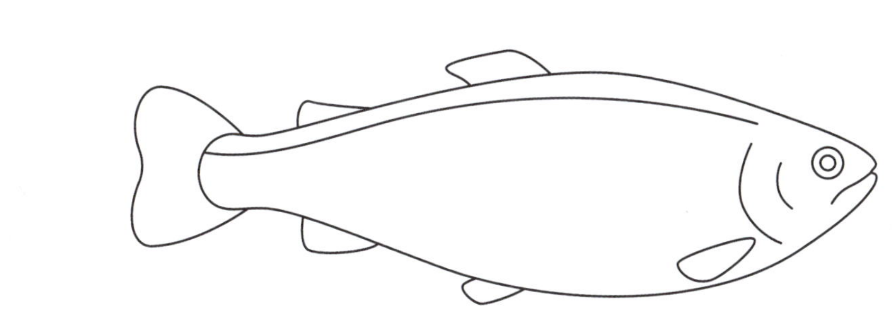

Drop-in joins

Learning intention: To practise drop-in joins

I am successful when I can:

- ☐ sit with my back straight
- ☐ hold my pen correctly
- ☐ position my paper
- ☐ drop the letters a, c, d, g and q into place.

Tip! The letters a, c, d, g and q are dropped into place after a diagonal join.

ea — The dropped-in letter touches the join here.

Practise your drop-in joins as you copy the letters and words below.

ed ec ad ac eq ca nd ma ic og eg ta

land sustain habitat adaptation demand adapt

total population animals bacteria decomposer change

Copy the words below, which relate to the Earth's ecosystems.

biosphere ________	communities ________
biomes ________	population ________
biodiversity ________	species ________

Horizontal joins

I am successful when I can:

- ☐ sit with my back straight
- ☐ hold my pen correctly
- ☐ position my paper
- ☐ use horizontal joins for the letters b, o, r, v and w.

Learning intention: To practise horizontal joins

slight dip
ou ba
slight dip

Practise your horizontal joins as you copy the letters, words and sentence below.

on oq vi fa rg ba od vo ok wo oo

of oa wr ol ro va oc ra ou wi

biomes without various warm survival wind

processes vigorous food organic own consumer cob

The Earth's ecosystems operate as a vibrant and interconnected web, where energy and nutrients flow through various trophic levels in food chains and food webs.

Self-assessment

Underline your smoothest join. Circle a join that needs more practice.

Tip! Remember to retrace the top of the letter when completing horizontal joins to anti-clockwise letters.

Practise your horizontal joins as you copy the letters, words and sentence below.

ro va oc wa rc fo od rg og oa

producer warmth forward variety destruction catalogue

Changes in one part of an ecosystem can have ripple effects for the plants and animals living there.

Choose from the items below and write the correct meaning next to each word.

An event that is interrupted by a problem	Involves using a lot of energy
The part of the Earth where there are living things	A substance that helps living things to grow

vigorous	
biosphere	
nutrient	
disruption	

Horizontal joins to e

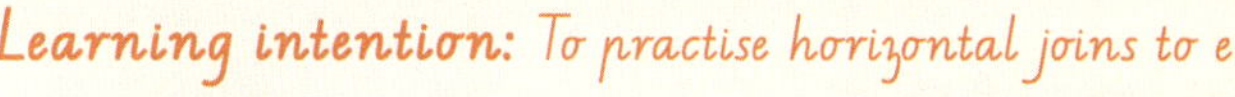

Tip! Remember that the horizontal join to e has a slightly lower dip.

Practise your joins to e as you copy the letters, words and sentences below.

Peer feedback

Ask a partner to review your work and provide feedback on how well you completed your joins.

Two stars (two things you did well)

One wish (one suggestion on something you can improve)

Joins to s

Learning intention: To practise horizontal joins to s

Remember to make the s shorter when you join to s diagonally.

es ts

Tip! When making a horizontal join to s, use the regular s.

rs

Practise your joins to s as you copy the letters, words and sentences below.

os rs ts ws es is as vs ns ms ds

layers leaves oceans shapes across regions

A variety of biomes exist around the world (for example, tropical rainforests or deserts). Each has its own unique characteristics.

Fine motor skills task: Follow the steps to sketch the landscape, then colour it in.

Consolidating

Copy the passage below.

A habitat is an environment that is the natural home for living things, such as animals and plants, where they can find food, water and shelter. This is where living things interact with each other and the physical environment. Habitats are diverse and are shaped by climate and geography, which affect the reliability of resources.

What kind of habitat is in your local area? Can you write three adjectives to describe where you live? For example, urban, rural or coastal, quiet or noisy, leafy or high-rise.

Self-assessment Draw a star next to your neatest writing.

Practise your keyboarding skills by typing this passage.

Assessment: Diagonal, drop-in and horizontal joins

Sort these letter pairs into the correct join group.

on	ac	ed	aq	in	wn	eg	ve	ib
ka	ee	oo	ol	ca	ig	ng	un	ui
ea	wi	ni	un	uc	sa	an	wa	it

Diagonal joins: ______________________

Drop-in joins: ______________________

Horizontal joins: ______________________

Practise your cursive handwriting as you copy the words and sentence below.

regions carbon critical global ocean oxygen science

It is important to protect the Earth's ecosystems by using responsible and sustainable resource management practices that will safeguard them for future generations.

Teacher feedback

Practise your keyboarding skills by typing this passage.

Revising fluency joins

Tip! Remember to slide the base of the s to create smooth fluency joins.

Fluency joins with s

Learning intention:
To practise fluency joins to make my writing smooth and fluent

s at the start of a word — su — Retrace the base of the letter.

horizontal join to s — us

diagonal join to s — as — modified s

Add fluency joins to the letter pairs and words below.

os so is es su si us sa so se

compost solar preserve sustain soil sanctuary seconds

Practise your fluency joins as you copy the sentences below.

It is important that people help preserve habitats to maintain the overall health of ecosystems. Adopting sustainable practices can help protect and preserve habitats by allowing plant and animal species to thrive.

Self-assessment Draw a star next to your smoothest writing.

Practise your keyboarding skills by typing this passage.

Word-building task

Practise your fluency joins as you write the different forms of each word below. The first one is done for you.

Base verb	Suffix -ed	Suffix -ing	Noun
protect	protected	protecting	protection
adapt			
interact			
conserve			
interfere			
reduce			
preserve			

Fine motor skills task: Help Cooper through the jungle maze to find the toucan. Be careful not to touch the edges or lift your pen.

Fluency joins with double s

Learning intention: To make a double s

I am successful when I can:

- ☐ sit with my back straight
- ☐ hold my pen correctly
- ☐ position my paper
- ☐ use fluency joins with double s.

When joining double s, a regular s is used after a horizontal join. A modified double s is used after diagonal joins.

Practise your fluency joins with double s as you copy the words below. Notice that the double s looks different when there is a horizontal join before it.

mossy possible process across gloss toss blossom grass

bliss less asset necessary success discuss essential albatross

Practise your fluency joins with double s as you copy the sentences below.

Successful wildlife habitats require careful management, ensuring that invasive flora and fauna (plants and animals) don't interfere with resources such as shelter, food and water.

Self-assessment Draw a star next to your best writing.

Practise your keyboarding skills by typing this passage.

Practising fluency joins

Practise your fluency joins as you copy the sentences below.

There are a range of different habitats around the world that support a wide variety of species, from the lush rainforests of the Amazon to the arid deserts across inland Australia. All animals and plants adapt to their particular habitat so they can survive. Whether it is the icy Arctic tundra or the vibrancy of the Great Barrier Reef, these environments support life on our planet.

Rewrite these words using fluency joins. Then colour in the rainforest.

vibrancy	______	supporting	______
survive	______	different	______
across	______	arid	______
species	______	life	______
variety	______	icy	______

Consolidating

Set a timer to see how long it takes you to write this paragraph on the lines below. Add your time to the first box below for your first try.

Grassland habitats are wide-open spaces containing grasses and smaller plants rather than large trees. There are grassland habitats on most continents, but they have different names. In Africa, they are called savannahs, whereas in North America they are called prairies. Grasslands are in the drier parts of a continent, usually between mountains and deserts.

Write the paragraph again on these lines, and note your time in the second box below.

Now type the passage on a computer. Add your time to the third box.

Time taken to copy text the first time:

Time taken to copy text the second time:

Time taken to type text:

Which way was quickest? Which one did you prefer? Discuss the benefits of handwriting and of typing with a classmate.

Assessment: Fluency joins

Practise your cursive handwriting and fluency joins as you copy the words below.

scrublands plants between spaces people

supply grasslands sustainable parts blissful

understandable sparse typically burning seasons

Rewrite this printed script sentence in your best joined cursive on the lines below.

The diverse habitats of the world allow for animals and plants of many varieties to flourish.

Write your own sentence in cursive. Try to use words that include a double s following a horizontal join and a diagonal join. See page 15 for ideas.

Teacher feedback

Speed loops and fluency

Learning intention:
To use speed loops to make my writing faster and more fluent, focusing on g, j, y and z

Speed loops for g, j, y and z

I am successful when I can:
- ☐ sit with my back straight
- ☐ hold my pen correctly
- ☐ position my paper
- ☐ use speed loops for fluency and speed.

g j y z

Speed loops from a tail letter cross at the baseline.

Practise your speed loops from g as you copy the letters and words below. (Remember that the letters g, j, y and z at the end of a word do not need a speed loop.)

ga ga ge ge gi gi go go gr gr gu gu

green growth gorgeous large glacier global grass

germinate region grove garden geology gully encourage

Practise your speed loops from j as you copy the letters and words below.

ja ja ja je je je ji ji ji jo jo jo ju ju ju

journey judging jubilant jungle jacaranda jabiru

Practise your speed loops from y as you copy the letters and words below.

ya ya ye ye yi yi yo yo yr yr yu yu

yacht yield youngest youth yearn skyrail yucca

Practise your speed loops for z as you copy the letters, words and sentences below.

za za za ze ze ze zi zi zi zy zy zl zl zz zz

breezy grazing zesty zebras zigzag blaze buzz hazy drizzle

Among the most distinctive animals on the African grasslands are black-and-white striped zebras. They enjoy grazing on the abundant vegetation.

Fine motor skills task: Follow the steps to sketch the zebra.

growing

speed loop

no speed loop

Tip!

Remember that when g, j, y and z are the final letters in a word, they do not need a speed loop because they are not joining to anything.

Practise your speed loops as you copy the words and sentences below.

ecology recycle drying gleaming organic juniper

juicy geothermal jagged agriculture mangrove layers

Wildflowers thrive in grasslands across the world, adding colour and attracting pollinators. They include bluebells, wild bergamot and grevilleas. A zoologist could explain that these wildflowers are not only attractive, but also crucial for the ecology of an area.

Fine motor skills task: Follow the steps to sketch the flower, then colour it in.

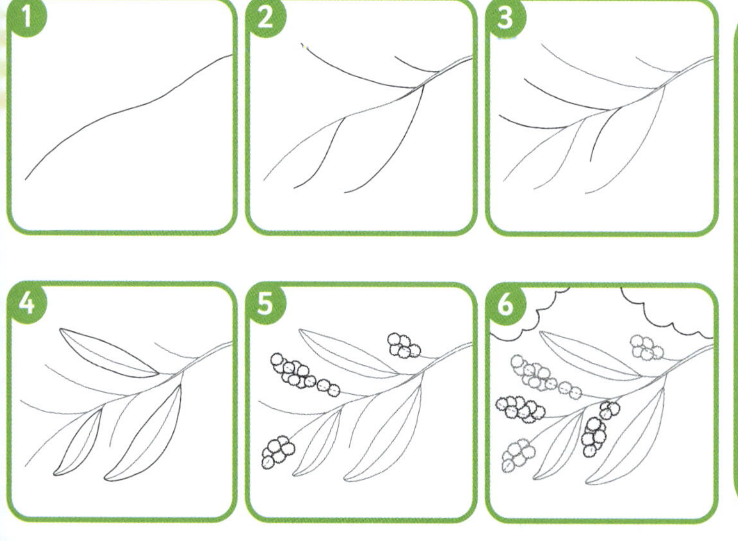

Speed loops for f

Learning intention: To use speed loops for the letter f

no loop over the first f — loops for the middle and end of words

for coffee diff

Tip! When forming f, use a speed loop to write more quickly. If a word starts with f, then it has a regular f at the start. If the word has an f in the middle or at the end, we use the loop to write faster.

Practise your speed loops for f as you copy the words and sentences below. Before you begin, colour the letter f in green if it's at the start of a word, or orange if it's a loop letter f in the middle or at the end of a word.

found features flaunt reef colourful fauna

rainfall fish rainforest effect footprint diff

Coral reefs are found in warm, shallow waters that are rich in biodiversity. They are home to coral colonies, colourful fish and other types of marine life. One of the most famous coral reefs is the Great Barrier Reef, on Australia's north-east coast. It is the largest coral-reef ecosystem in the world and was declared a World Heritage Area in 1981.

Self-assessment Circle the words with your best speed loops for f.

OXFORD UNIVERSITY PRESS

In cursive handwriting, copy these commonly confused words and their definitions.

affect (verb)	to produce a change in something
effect (noun)	a result of something
effect (verb) (quite rare)	to make something happen

Practise your speed loops as you copy the sentences below. Then colour in the seascape.

Warmer ocean waters affect coral reefs, leading to coral bleaching.

The oil spill had an adverse effect on marine life.

The minister tried to effect a change in environmental policy.

Speed loops for tall letters

Learning intention: To use speed loops for tall letters

b f h k l

I am successful when I can:

- ☐ sit with my back straight
- ☐ hold my pen correctly
- ☐ position my paper
- ☐ use speed loops for forming the letters b, f, h, k and l.

Practise your neatest writing as you copy the letters, words and sentences below.

ab eb ak lk ah oh al el ol ul sl cl ch sh wh

research zebu alpine waterfall brisk cobweb elk

peak brink altitudes alpaca elevation herbivores harsh

From snow-capped peaks to alpine valleys, mountain habitats

are known for their dramatic landscapes and unique features.

These habitats are characterised by their elevation and cold climate.

This photo is of Aoraki (Mt Cook). At 3754 metres, it is Aotearoa/

New Zealand's highest mountain and

a favourite with mountain-climbers.

Add loops when joining to b, f, h, k or l.

Tip! The letters b, f, h, k and l do not need a speed loop when they appear at the start of a word.

Practise your speed loops as you copy the sentences below.

Snow leopards are elusive big cats that live in the mountainous regions of Central and South Asia. They have spotted coats that provide excellent camouflage in the rocky, snowy mountain ranges. Snow leopards have adapted to cold climates with their dense fur and furry paws for insulation.

Use coloured pencils to colour in the different shapes in the snow leopard.

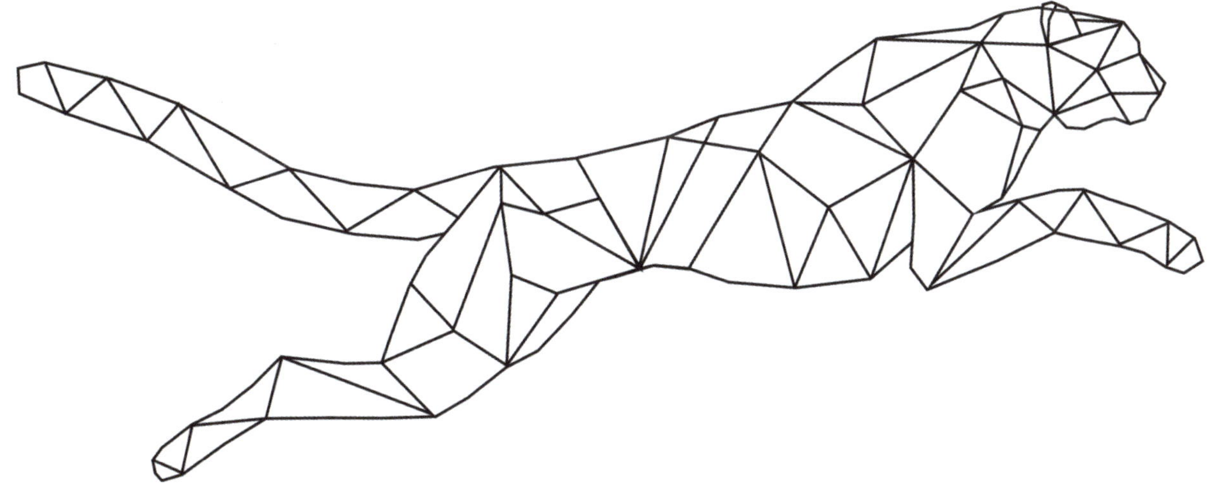

Fluency and speed

Learning intention: To practise fluency and speed

I am successful when I can:

- ☐ sit with my back straight
- ☐ hold my pen correctly
- ☐ position my paper
- ☐ use speed loops to increase fluency and speed.

Tip! It is important to practise fluency in handwriting so that you can write in an easy and automatic way.

Practise your speed loops as you copy the sentences. Try to increase your speed as you go.

Alpacas and llamas are native to the Andes Mountains of South America.

Sometimes confused with alpacas, llamas are larger, feistier and less woolly.

Llamas have an elongated face with large, expressive eyes and banana-shaped ears.

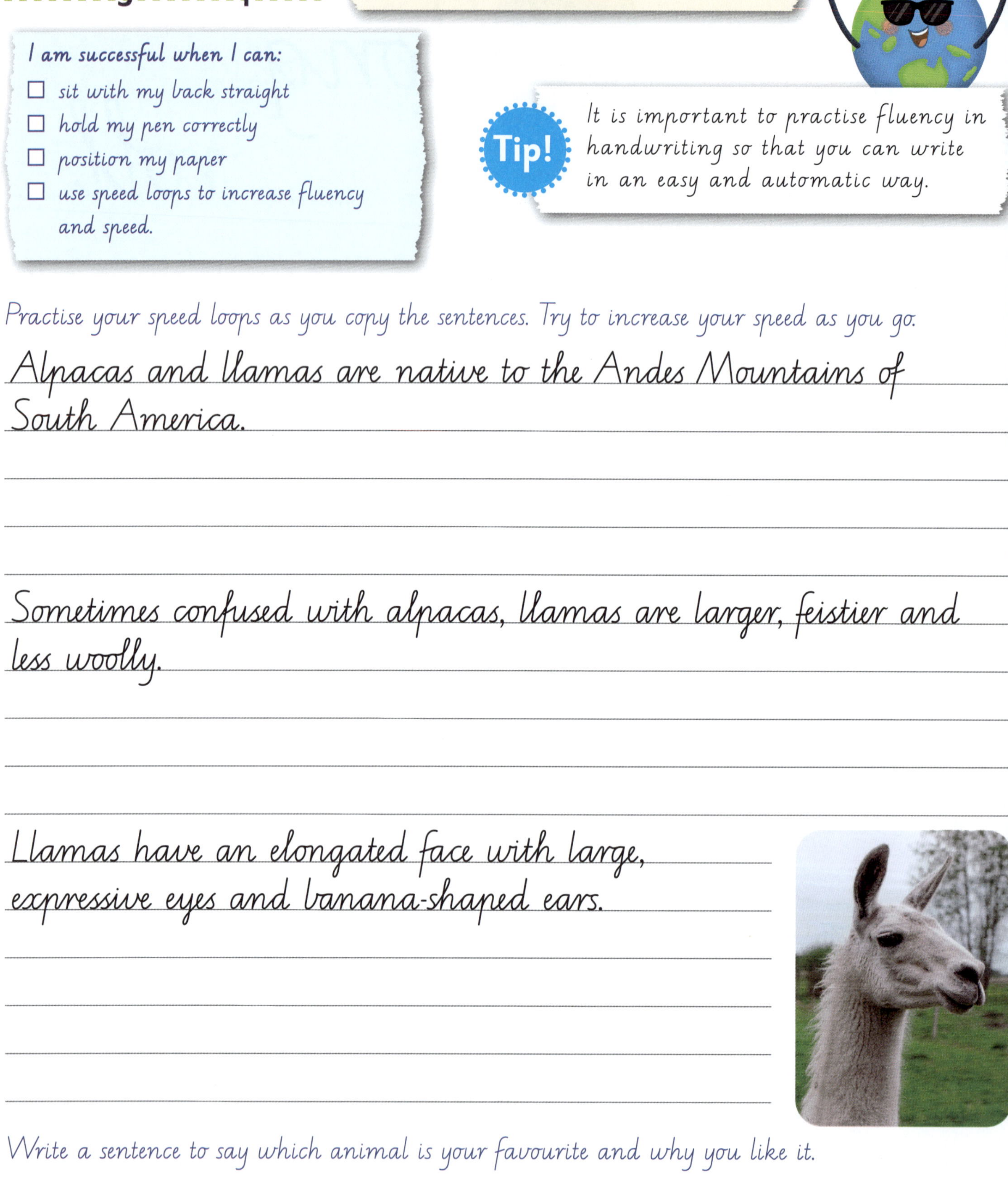

Write a sentence to say which animal is your favourite and why you like it.

Practise your speed loops as you copy the words three times. Try to increase your speed in the second and third rows.

blossom branch bloom high higher highest

like lively large bubble kicker skate

Practise your speed loops as you copy the words below.

launch		landmarks	
track		harshly	
brook		natural	
creek		landform	
sadly		skilled	
lagoon		livelihood	
breezily		hillside	
effortless		broken	
hollow		loosely	
wetland		horizon	
healthy		rainforest	

Consolidating

Practise your cursive handwriting and speed loops as you copy the sentences below.

Tundra habitats are challenging environments, shaped by extreme climates, and are typically found near the Earth's polar regions. They are very cold places that experience long winters, with temperatures often below freezing. There are fewer species that live in this environment, compared to other ecosystems, due to the extreme conditions.

Peer feedback

Ask a partner to review your work and provide feedback on how well you completed your joins.

Two stars *(two things you did well)*

One wish *(one suggestion on something you can improve)*

Assessment: Speed loops

Practise your speed loops as you copy the poem below. This is the first verse of the poem. You can search for it online if you would like to read the rest of the poem.

"I wandered lonely as a cloud"

by William Wordsworth

I wandered lonely as a cloud
That floats on high o'er vales and hills,
When all at once I saw a crowd,
A host, of golden daffodils;
Beside the lake, beneath the trees,
Fluttering and dancing in the breeze.

Teacher feedback

Legibility

Printing

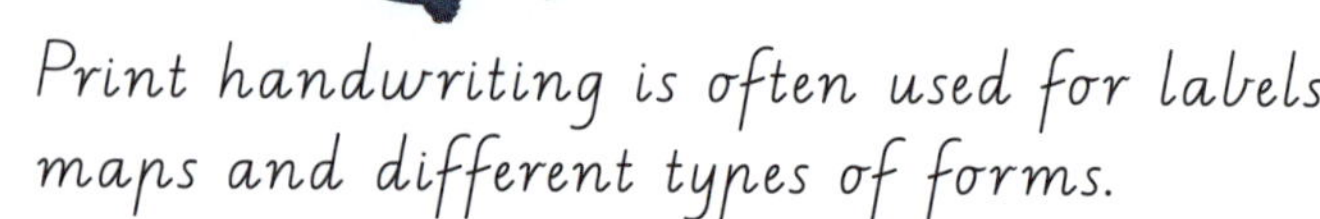

Print each word neatly.

toucan polar bear kangaroo stingray scorpion

crocodile green sea turtle Arctic fox camel

cassowary lion horned lizard zebra panther

From the list above, write the name of one of the animals that lives in these habitats. Print neatly.

Arctic tundra ______ desert ______

grassland ______ coral reef ______

rainforest ______ wetland ______

Fine motor skills task: Follow the steps to sketch the bear, then colour it in.

OXFORD UNIVERSITY PRESS

Capital letters

Practise your capital letters as you print the names of the continents and oceans on the map.

South America

Antarctica

North America

Australia

Africa

Europe

Asia

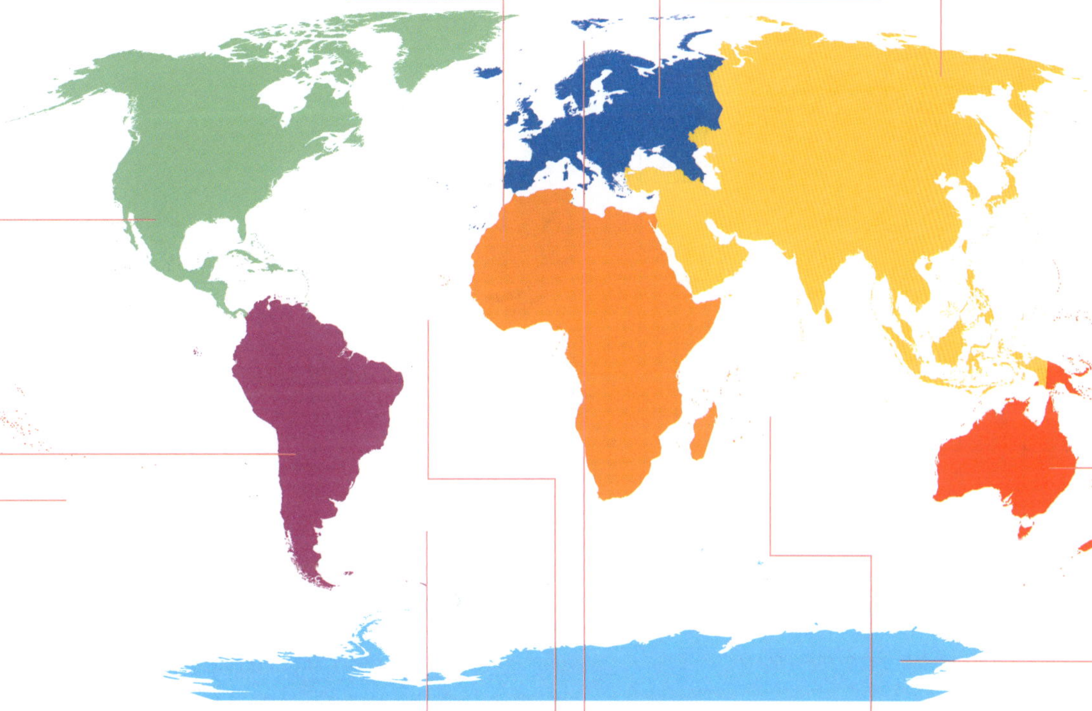

Southern Ocean

Indiun Ocean

Atlantic Ocean

Arctic Ocean

Pacific Ocean

Practise your capital letters as you complete the crossword about animals.

Tip! The numbers in brackets after the clues are the number of letters in the answer. If there are two words, then there are two numbers.

Across

2 Rainforest animal that moves very slowly (5)

7 Dog-like carnivore of Africa and Asia (5)

8 One of Australia's deadliest reptiles (5, 5)

9 Wool comes from this animal (5)

11 Mammal with long neck (7)

13 Swings through the trees (6)

Down

1 Some are free range, and others live caged (8)

3 Biggest mammal on Earth (4, 5)

4 Black jungle cat (7)

5 Big cat with stripes (5)

6 Deadly desert arachnid (8)

8 Colourful insect (9)

10 Considered the king of the jungle (4)

12 Common farm animal (3)

If you need some hints, your teacher has the answers to the crossword in the Teacher Resource material on Oxford Owl.

OXFORD UNIVERSITY PRESS

Spacing

Why is it important to practise spacing in handwriting?

Tip! Spacing is important because it helps to make your writing easier to read. Even letter spacing makes your writing more legible.

Tick the sentence that is most evenly spaced.

Writing that is evenly spaced is easier to read. ☐

Writing that is evenly spaced is easier to read. ☐

Writing that is evenly spaced is easier to read. ☐

Copy the sentence below twice and try to develop an even spacing between letters.

Rainforests are some of the most intricate ecosystems on Earth.

Copy the sentences below twice, then use a highlighter pen to highlight the line with the best word spacing.

Rainforests are lush habitats found in tropical regions near the

equator. They are characterised by lots of rainfall and year-round

warmth, creating excellent conditions for a wide variety of plants

and animals.

Size

tropical tRopiCal

even letter size uneven letter size

Tip! Keeping your letters an even size is an important skill to master. It will help increase your fluency.

Practise consistent letter size and spacing as you copy the sentences below.

There are two types of rainforest: tropical and temperate. They have distinct features that make them unique to their location and climate. Temperate rainforests are cooler than tropical rainforests. A temperate rainforest in Australia is Dandenong Ranges National Park in Victoria. Tropical rainforests are found closer to the equator and in countries across South and Central America, Africa and South-East Asia. A famous Australian tropical rainforest is the Daintree in Queensland.

Self-assessment Draw a star next to the line with the most consistent letter size.

Practise your keyboarding skills by typing this passage.

Slope

Tip! Having a consistent slope to your writing will help to make your writing more fluent and legible. Using a slight slope to the right makes it easier to control your pen and also makes it easier to join letters.

Write this word five times, using the slope lines as a guide.

equator

Circle the words with an inconsistent slope. Then, write all of the words using a consistent slope.

temperate warm emergent coasts

canopy dense rainfall climate

Practise a consistent slope as you copy the sentences below.

The hallmark of a rainforest is its towering trees, which form a multi-layered canopy. Tropical rainforests are home to numerous species of animals and plants. Although temperate rainforests have fewer plant and animal species, they are home to many birds, amphibians, insects, reptiles and large mammals.

Labelling

The layers of a tropical rainforest are shown below. Next to each heading, add dot points describing each layer. You may want to do some online research before you begin. The first one is done for you. Print neatly.

Emergent layer
- towering trees
- dense canopy below
- abundant direct sunlight
- home to birds and animals, such as parrots, monkeys and eagles

Canopy layer
-
-
-
-

Understorey layer
-
-
-
-

Forest floor
-
-
-
-

Using your dot points, write a descriptive sentence about a rainforest in cursive handwriting.

Practising size, spacing and slope

Learning intention:

To practise maintaining consistent size, spacing and slope in handwriting

I am successful when I can:

- ☐ keep my letter size, spacing and slope even.

ractise your speed loops as you copy the entences below.

A unique feature of a rainforest

s its towering trees, which form

he canopy. These trees can reach

taggering heights, with emergent

rees piercing through the canopy

to receive maximum sunlight. The

canopy itself creates a dense and

shaded environment beneath it.

Fine motor skills task: Draw two of your favourite trees, then colour them in.

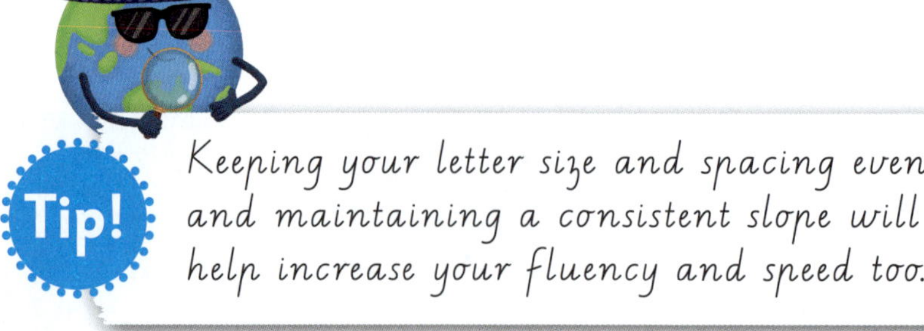

Tip! Keeping your letter size and spacing even and maintaining a consistent slope will help increase your fluency and speed too.

Practise your cursive handwriting as you copy the sentences below.

Rainforests are home to a multitude of animals and plants. Rainforests support a web of interconnected species, each playing a role in the balance and functioning of this intricate ecosystem. Some species that live in rainforests include monkeys, sloths, orangutans, gorillas, frogs and chameleons.

Finish the scene by adding the chameleon's surroundings in a rainforest.

Fluency

These words are often misspelt. Practise your cursive handwriting and speed loops as you copy them.

calendar fulfil separate maintenance quiet

beautiful experience receive privilege Arctic

achieve accommodate fascinating definitely foreign

Word-building task

In cursive handwriting, add the morphographs (word parts) together. The first one is done for you.

Remember to change the y to an i before adding the suffix. We usually drop the e before adding a suffix.

create + ive = creative

peace + ful + ly = __________

pro + port + ion = __________

un + ex + plain + ed = __________

re + late + ion = __________

noise + y + ness = __________

un + like + ly + ness = __________

re + cent + ly = __________

in + cure + able = __________

city + es = __________

room + y + ness = __________

The rainforest is home to some fascinating and unique birds. Practise your speed, fluency and cursive handwriting as you copy the sentences on this page and the next.

Cassowary

Cassowaries are large, flightless birds that are native to the

rainforests of north-eastern Australia and New Guinea. They have

striking blue facial skin and a helmet-like casque on their heads.

The casque protects the cassowary as it moves through dense forest.

Cassowaries have three-toed feet with a sharp claw on the inner

toe that helps them dig for food and ward off predators.

Scarlet macaw

An iconic bird that is native to the rainforests of Central and South America is the scarlet macaw. Known for its vibrant colours, it spends much of its time in the canopy. Scarlet macaws are beautiful, large parrots and can measure up to 83 cm from beak to tail.

Toucan

Found in the rainforests of Central and South America, toucans have an unusual appearance. Their most distinctive feature is their large and colourful bill.

Copy this definition of an adverb.

An adverb is a word that modifies or describes a verb, adjective or another adverb.

Copy the sentence below. Then use a highlighter pen to highlight the adverbs.

Vividly coloured toucans soar gracefully through the dense rainforest canopy.

Copy these adverbs.

kindly	carefully	warmly	safely
beautifully	politely	bravely	gracefully
honestly	vividly	quickly	always
certainly	softly	foolishly	usually

In cursive handwriting, write about a bird of the rainforest and describe its behaviour. Include at least three adverbs and use complete sentences.

Consolidating

Practise your speed and fluency as you copy the sentences below.

Animals and plants have adapted to survive in their environment over many years. This has helped them to improve their chances of survival. An "adaptation" is a feature of a living thing that helps it adjust to its habitat. For example, chameleons are able to change colour. They do this to blend in with their surroundings, regulate their body temperature or attract a potential mate. Koalas have adapted to eat only eucalyptus leaves. This gives them an advantage because the leaves are toxic to most animals.

Fine motor skills task: Follow the steps to sketch the bird, then colour it in.

Self-assessment Draw a star next to the line with the most consistent letter size.

Practise your keyboarding skills by typing this passage.

Speed test

It is important to master fluent and speedy handwriting. Practising your speed in forming letters and words can help to improve overall proficiency.

Read the sentence and try to remember it. Write out the sentence as many times as you can within two minutes using fluency joins and speed loops.

Animals can be classified into different groups: mammals, birds, reptiles, amphibians, invertebrates and fish.

Self-assessment

Rate your fluency (could you write smoothly and without much effort?)

Rate your legibility (can your writing be easily read by someone else?)

Developing a style

Tip!

Handwriting can be adjusted to suit the purpose. When you are taking notes, you might use speed loops to ensure your writing is quick. For labelling maps or filling out forms, you would use print handwriting. If you are creating a presentation or a document for a special occasion, you might add more flourishes to your handwriting.

Trace and then copy the flourished letters below.

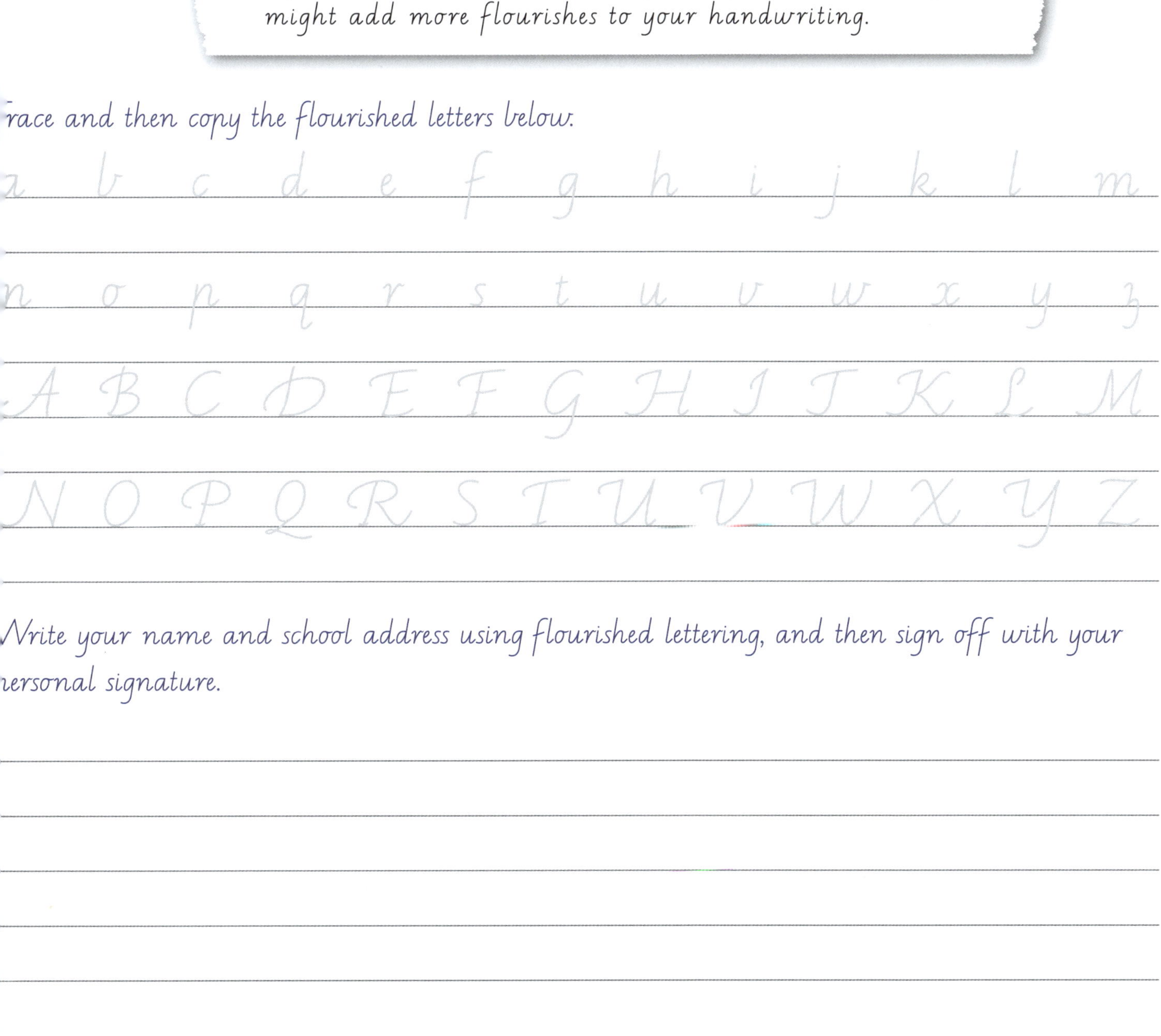

Write your name and school address using flourished lettering, and then sign off with your personal signature.

Signature: ______________________

Note-taking

Note-taking is an important skill to learn. Taking notes helps to keep a record of information that you have read or listened to. Sometimes, note-taking may not be very neat, but it should still be legible.

Complete some research on an animal you would like to learn more about. Find out about its appearance, diet, habitat and behaviour.

1. Use the listed websites to help you research.
2. Write your notes in the box below.

Useful sources of information

- Your school library
- https://kids.nationalgeographic.com/animals
- https://animalfactguide.com
- https://www.softschools.com/facts/animals

Your note-taking should include the following information.

- Appearance – what does your animal look like?
- Behaviour – how does it move and behave?
- Diet – what does it eat?
- Habitat – where does it live?

Consolidating

Tip! Start with a compelling introduction that provides a brief overview of your chosen animal and why it's interesting or important. Use your best cursive handwriting, ensuring that your work is neat and legible.

Writing activity

Use your research and your notes to write an engaging and informative paragraph about your chosen animal.

Draw your chosen animal.

Practise your keyboarding skills by typing your text.

Assessment: Legibility

Practise your speed loops and cursive handwriting as you copy the sentences below.

Many species around the world are facing the threat of extinction due to habitat loss, climate change and other human-related factors. Rainforest species are under enormous threat, mainly due t habitat loss and illegal poaching. Some of the endangered species found in rainforests include orangutans, pygmy elephants, leopard and gorillas. Conservation efforts are crucial to protect these species and preserve the delicate balance of rainforest ecosystems.

Teacher feedback